Federico Beltran Masses

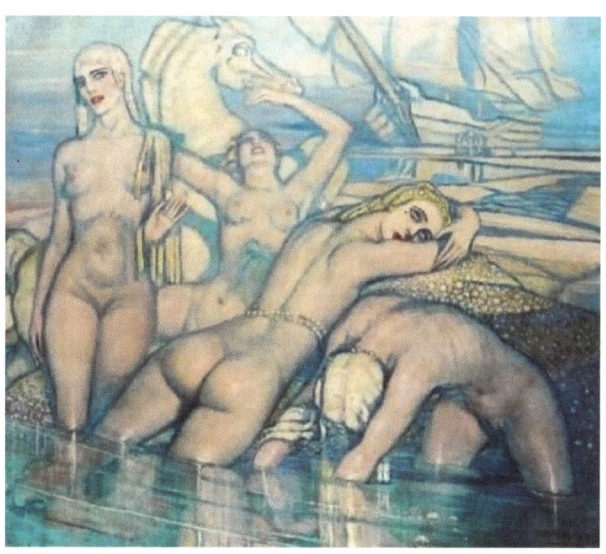

Edited by Lacey Belinda Smith

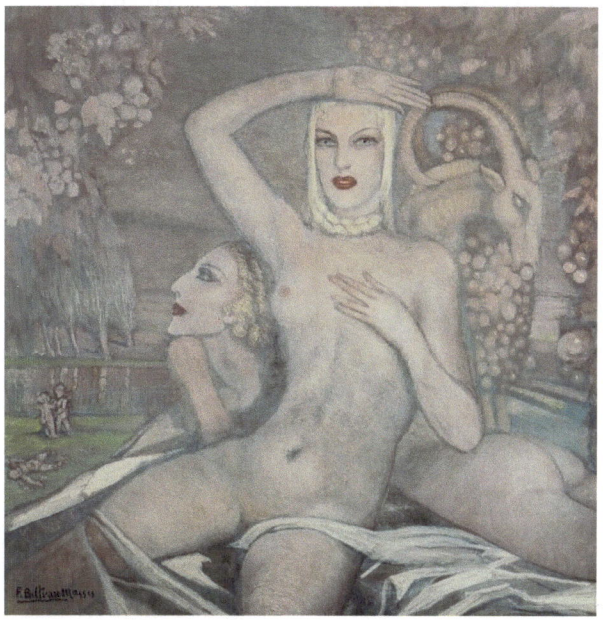

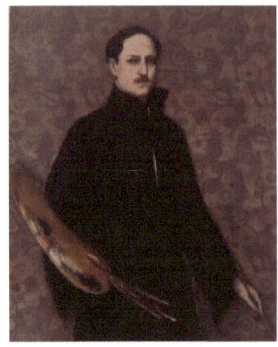

Self-portrait of Federico Beltran Masses

Federico Armando Beltran Masses (1885–1949) was born in Guaira de la Melena, Cuba when it was still a colony of Spain. His family was of Catalan origin. He spent his youth in Barcelona where he started to train as an artist in the well-known school Llotja. Later he went to live in Madrid where he studied under Sorolla at the Barcelona Academy of Fine Art. It was there where he attained national recognition after King Alfonso XIII acquired a work at the painter's first exhibition. He married Irene Narezo Dragoné, a painter like himself, who came from a wealthy and distinguished family. In 1916 Masses, like Picasso, and Ruiz, moved to Paris. He would live there for the next thirty years. In 1946 he abandoned Paris and went back to Barcelona, where he died in 1949.

Federico Beltran Masses often painted his subjects in exotic roles centring on the sensuality of the female form which is the subject of

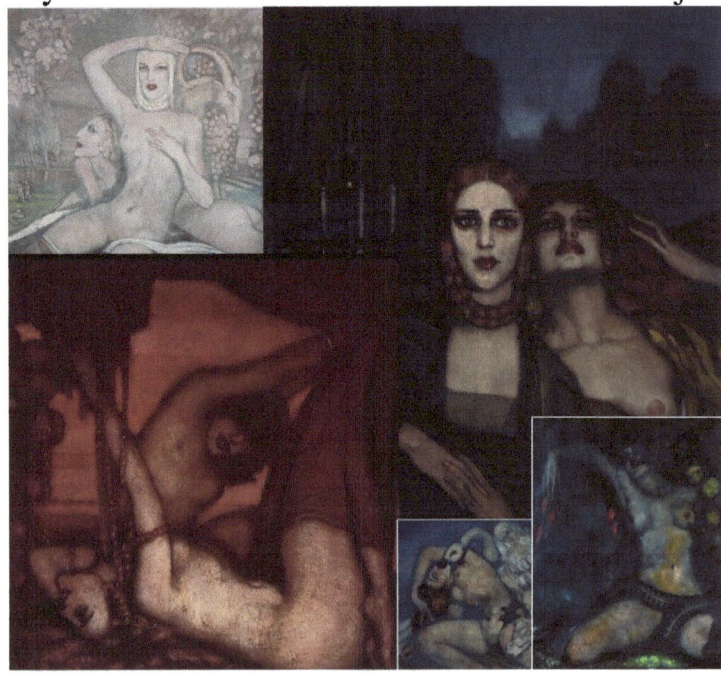

this present work.

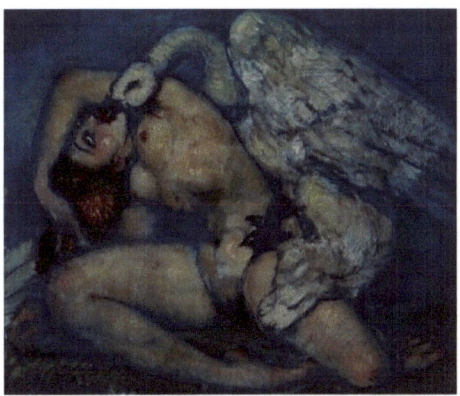

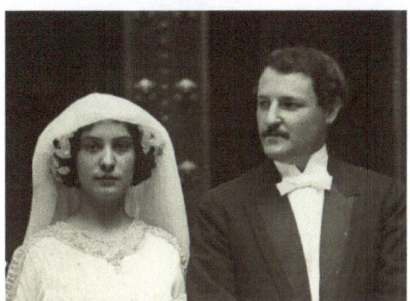

Beltran Masses and Irene Narezo Dragoné's wedding

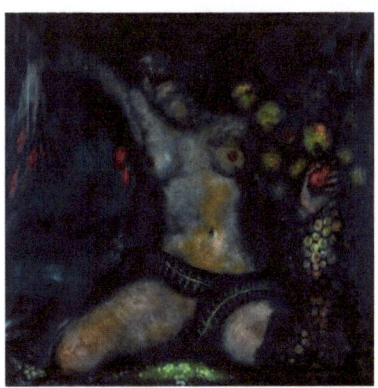

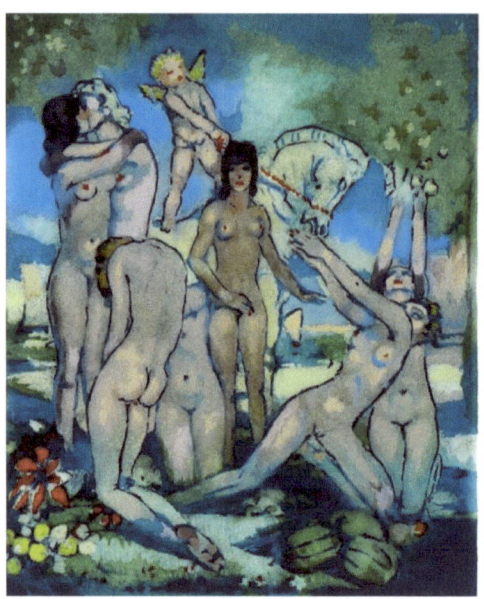

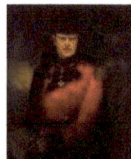

Self-portrait of Federico Beltran Masses

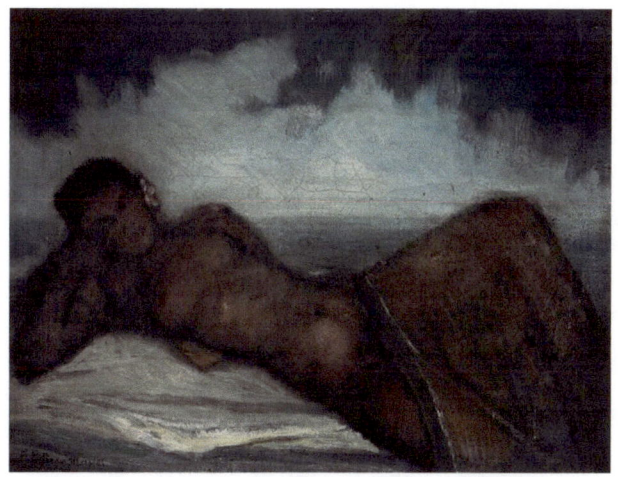

Vahiné alanguie

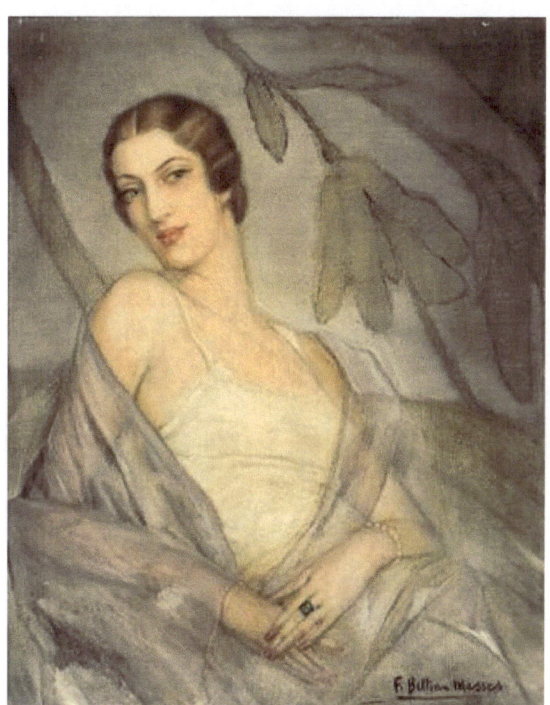

Una joven

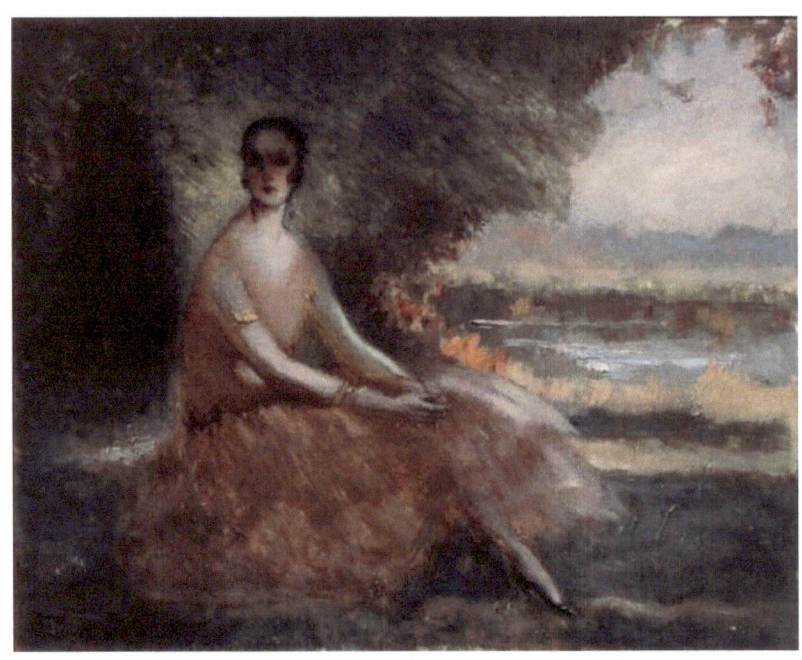

Elégante assise près de l'étang

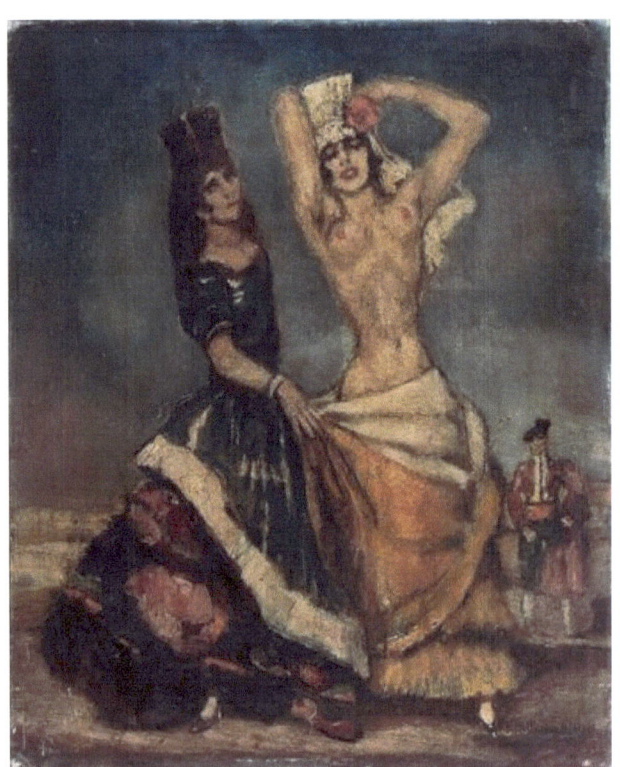

Danseuse de Flamenco

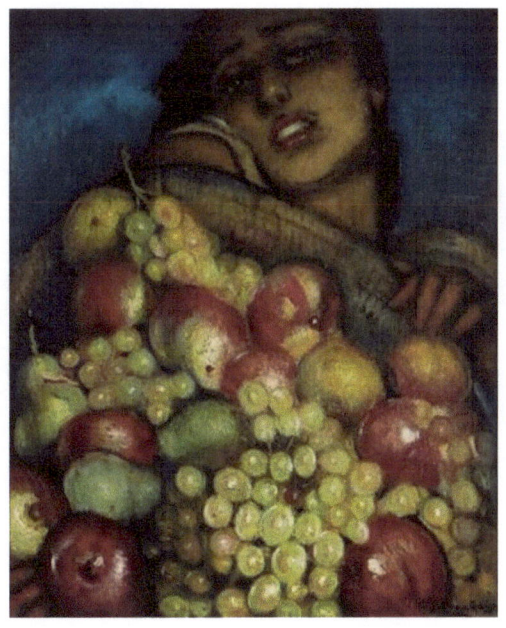

Fruitas

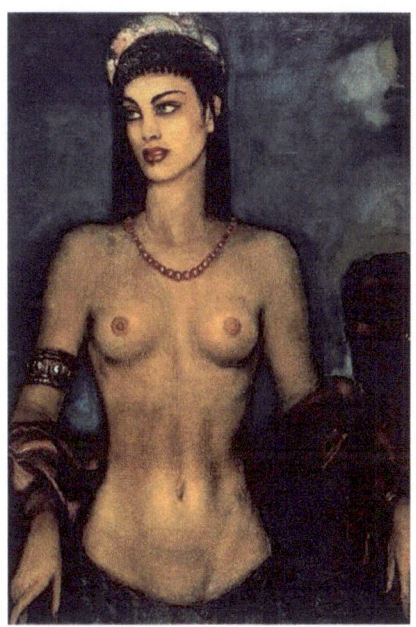

Salome

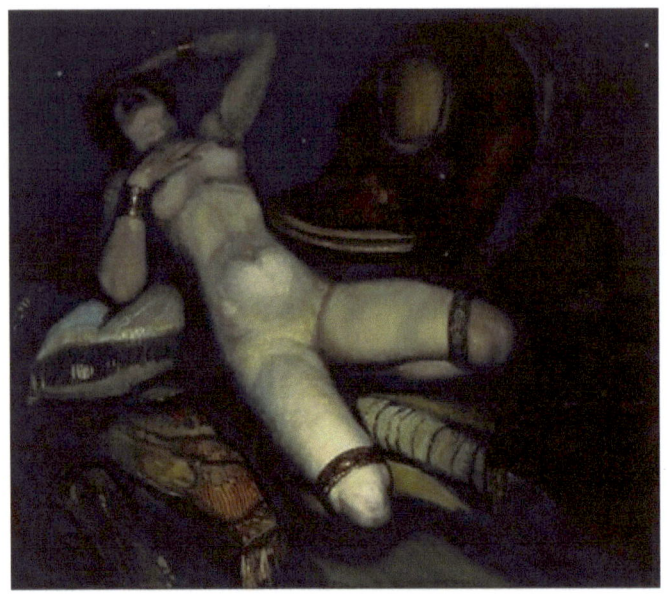

Salomé, 1918

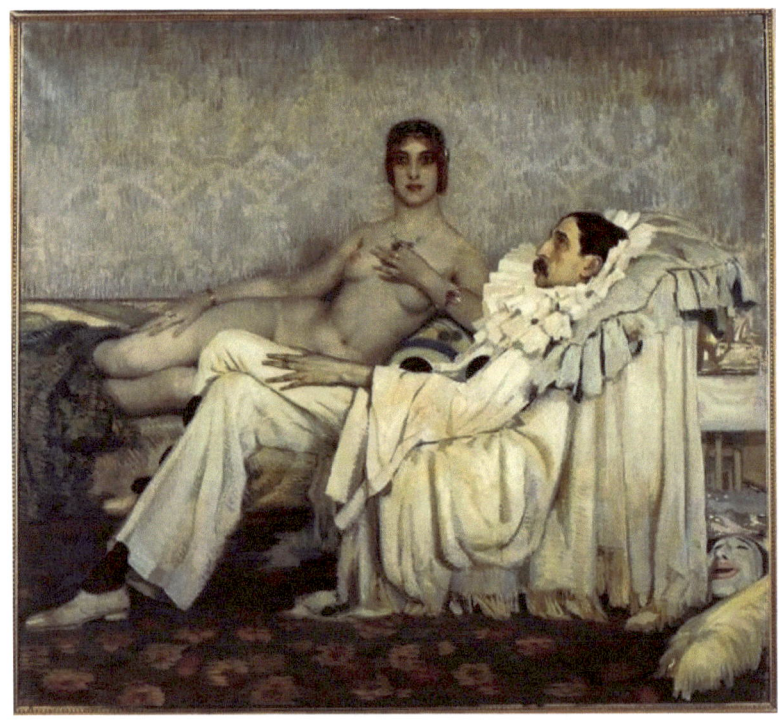

Pierrot y Colombia

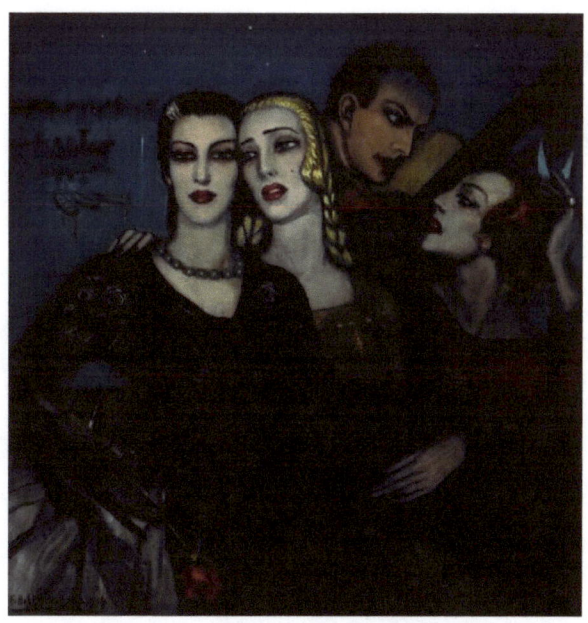

Tres para uno (Three for one)

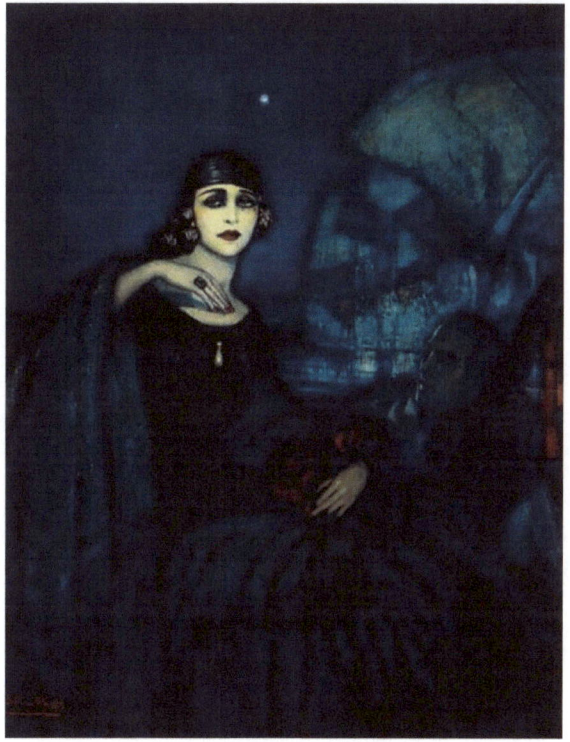

Pola Negri and Rudolph Valentino

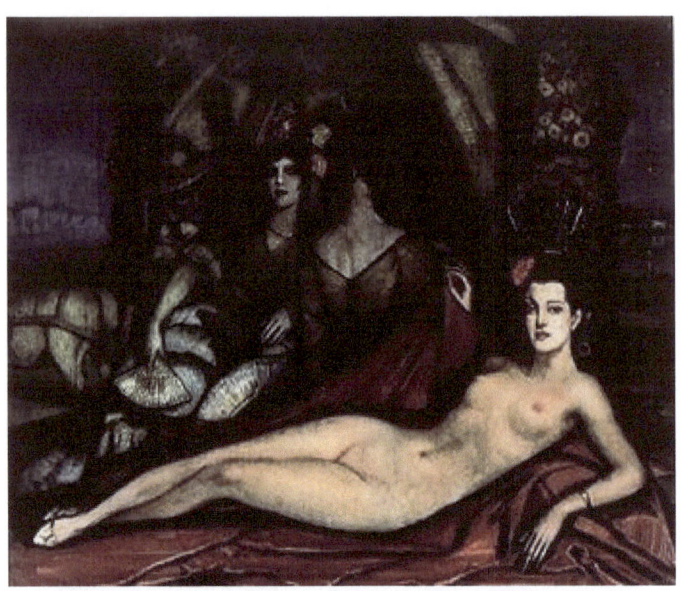

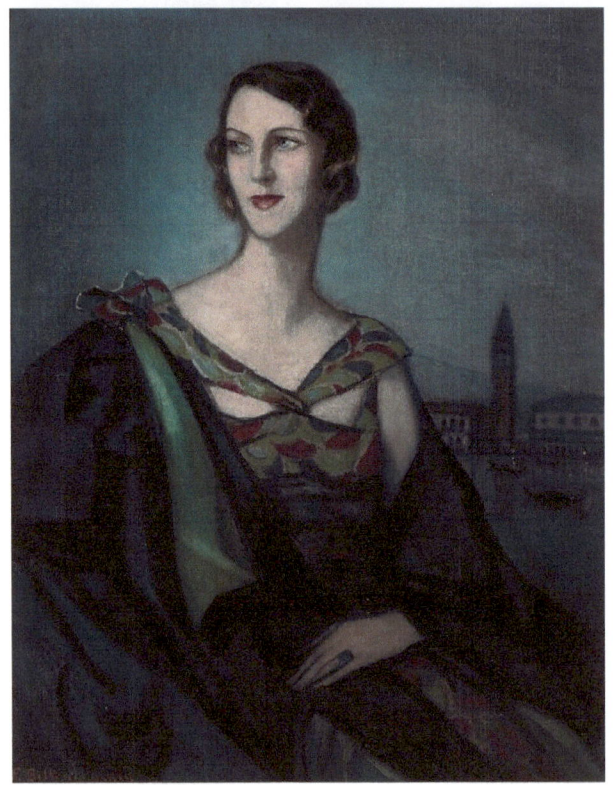

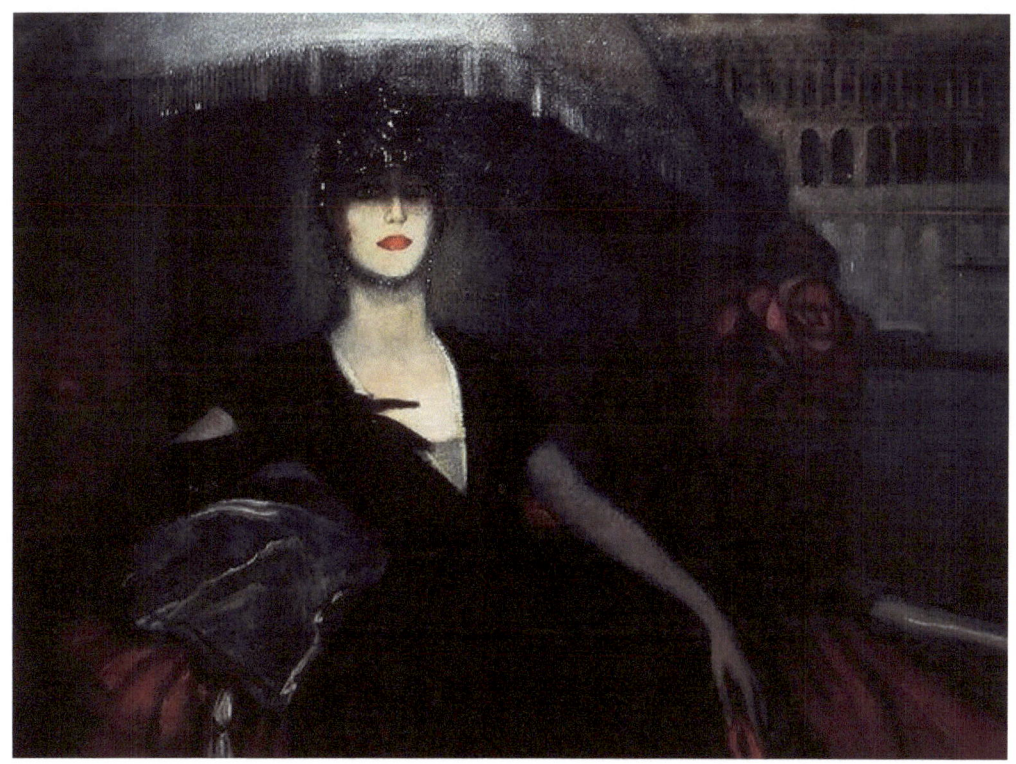

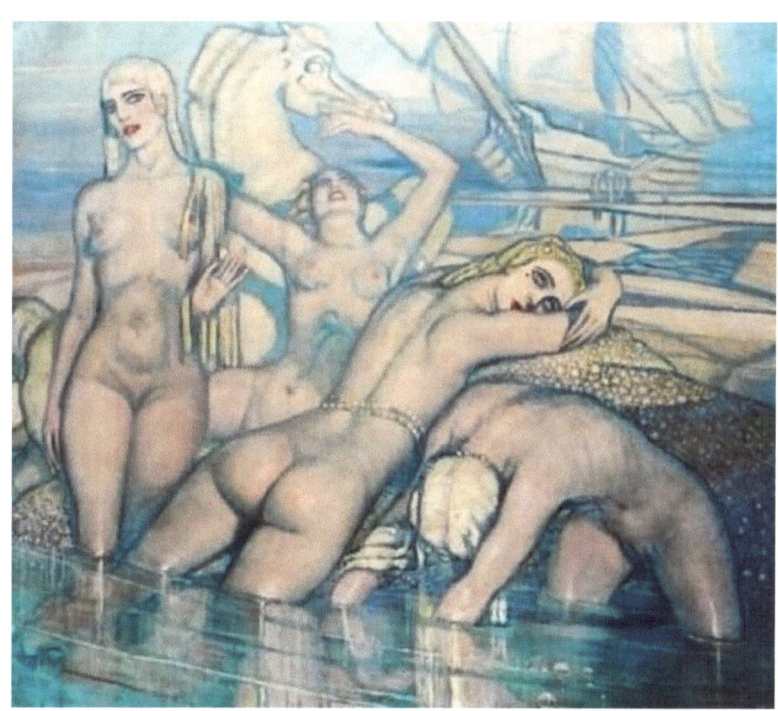

Perlas

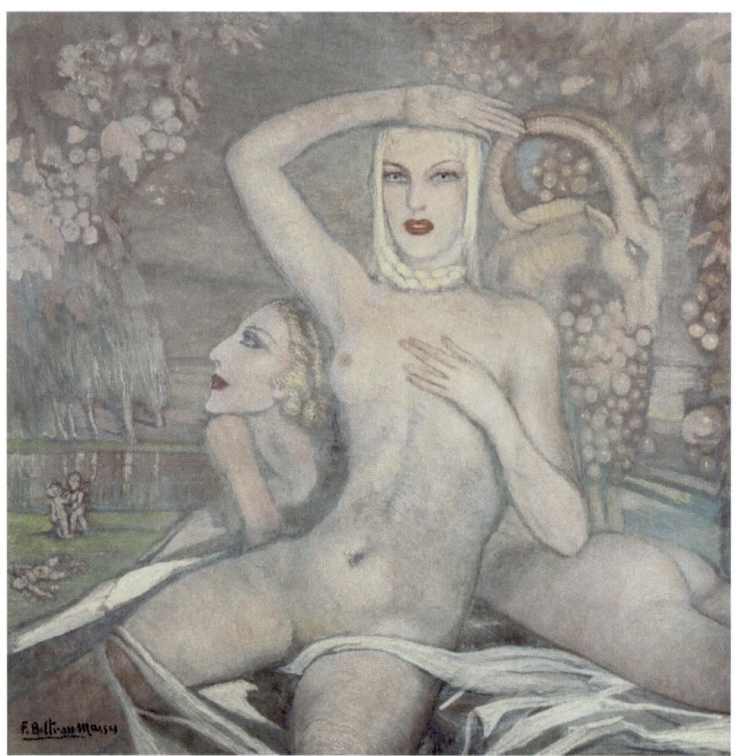

Alba

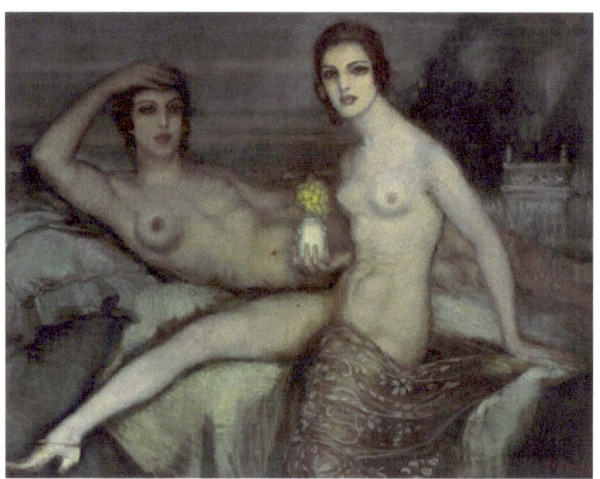

Siemprevivas

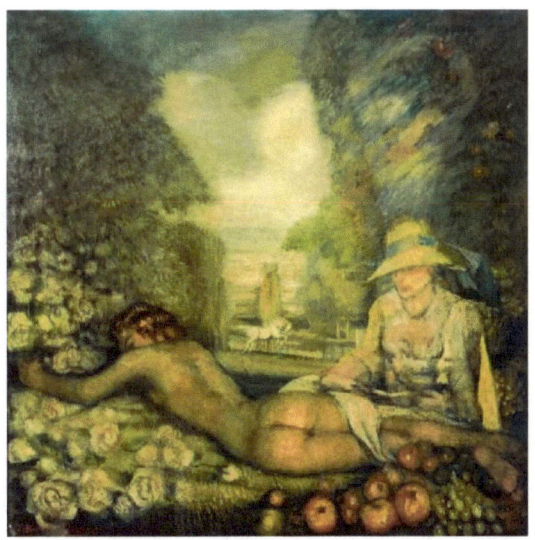

El sueño d'Eva

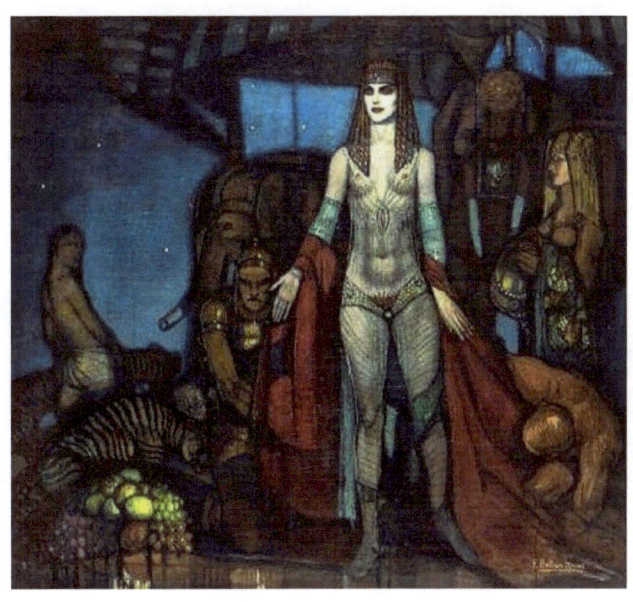

La Reina de Saba

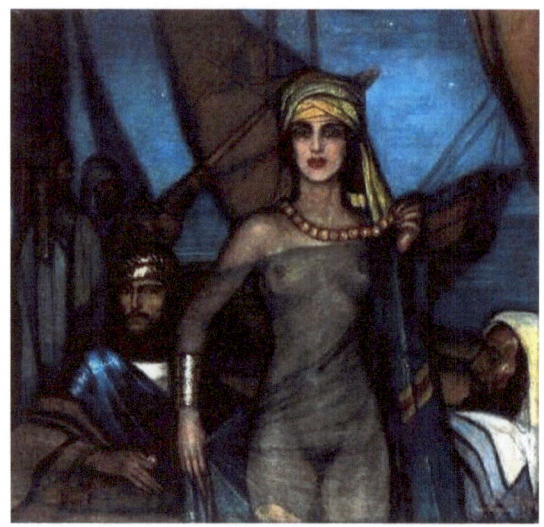

Mercado del Ambar

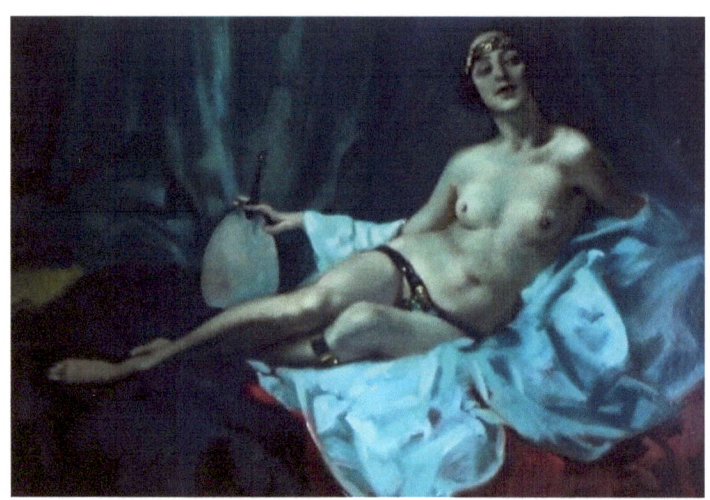

Mujer recostada

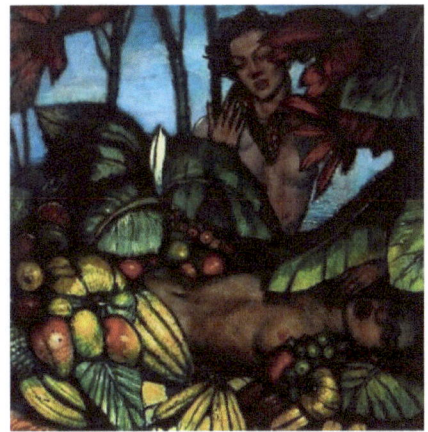

Tropical--1929

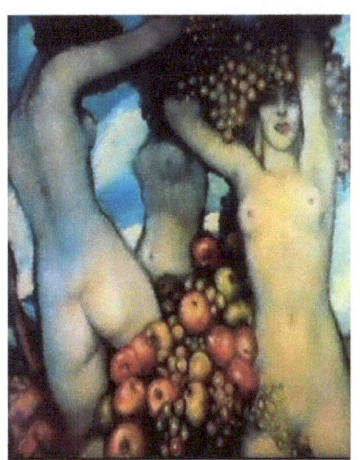

Uvas y manzanas

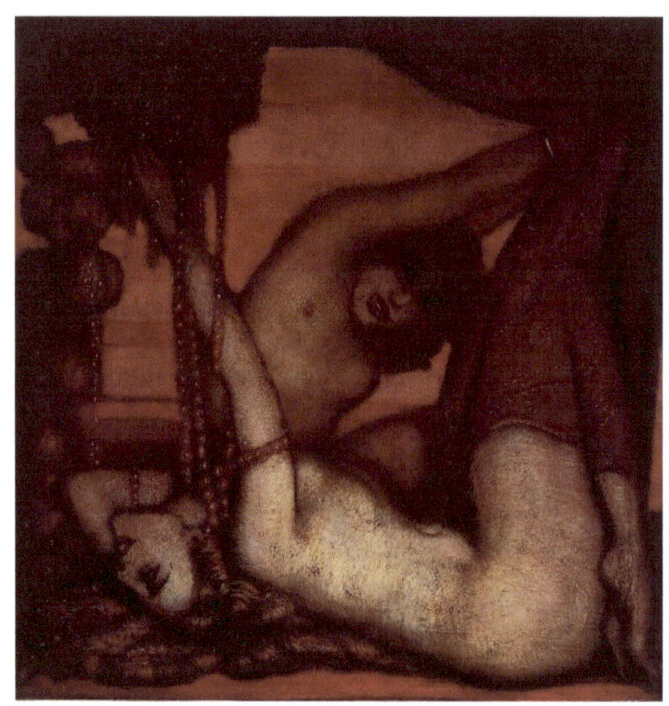

El Rubi

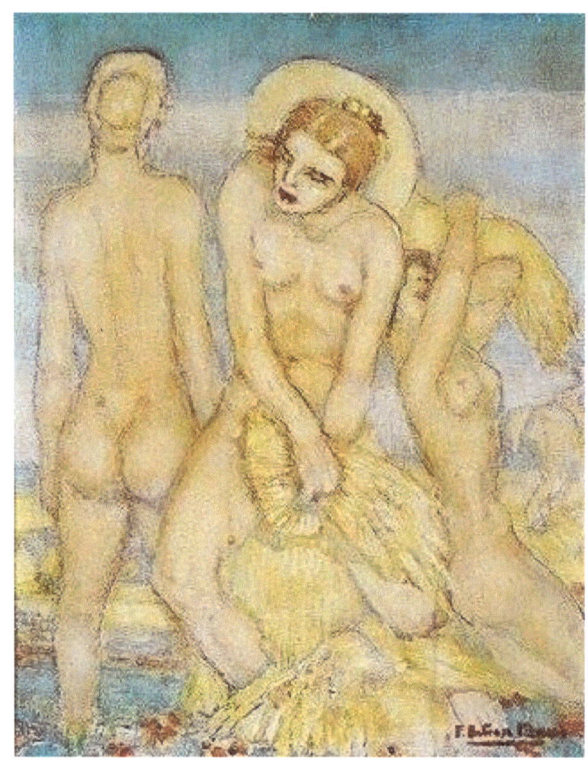

Verano

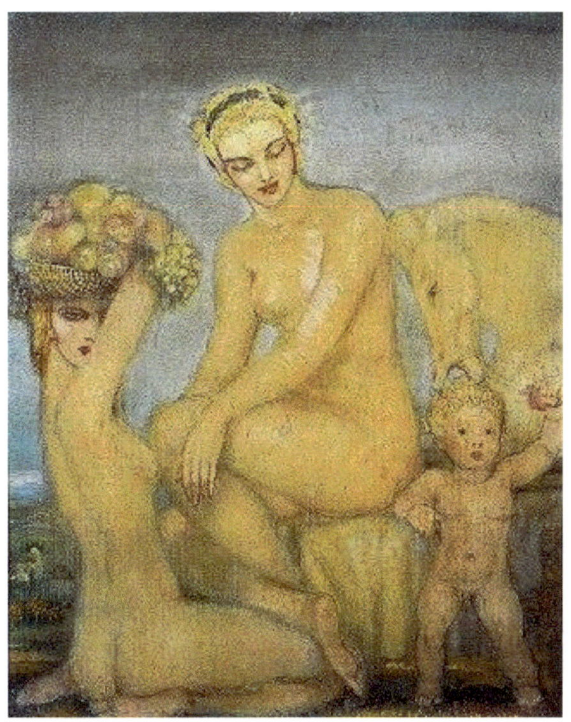

Otoño

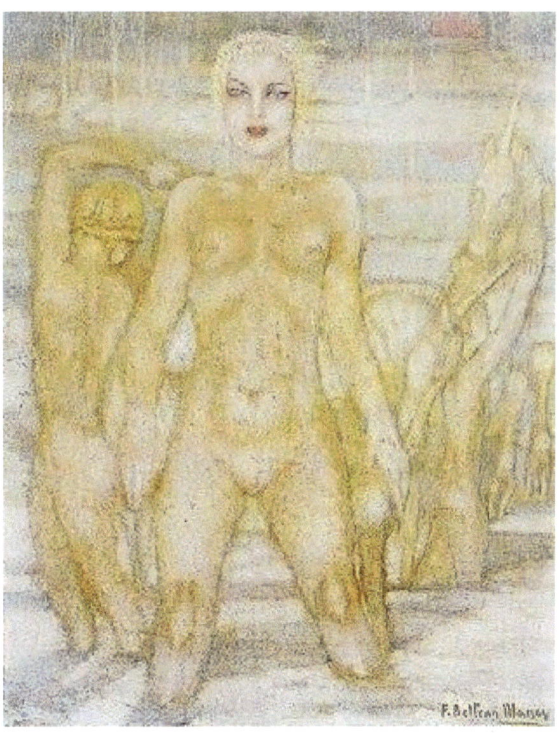

Inverno

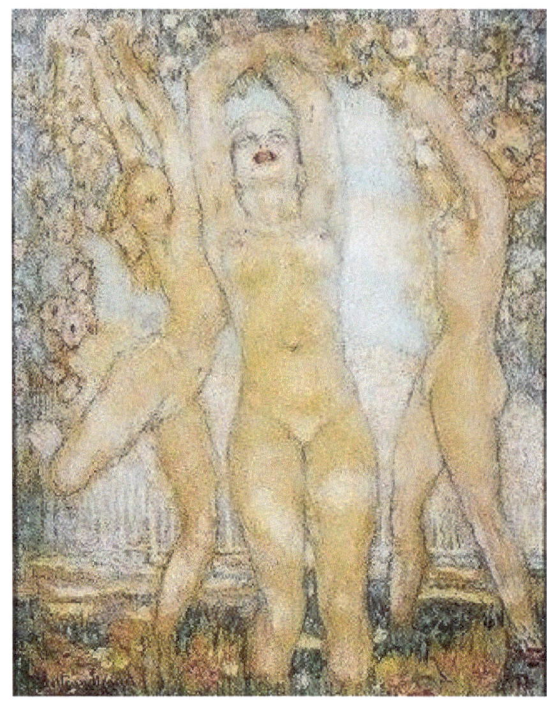

Spring

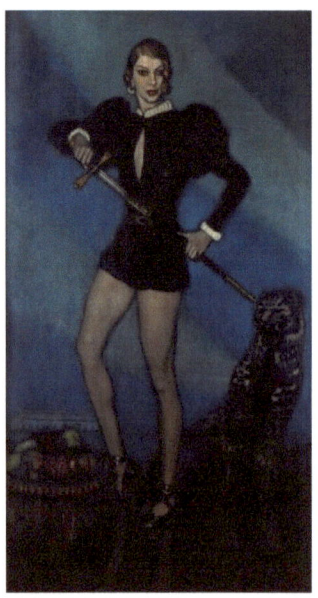

Portrait of the Ballets Russes dancer Alicia Nikitina-- 1929

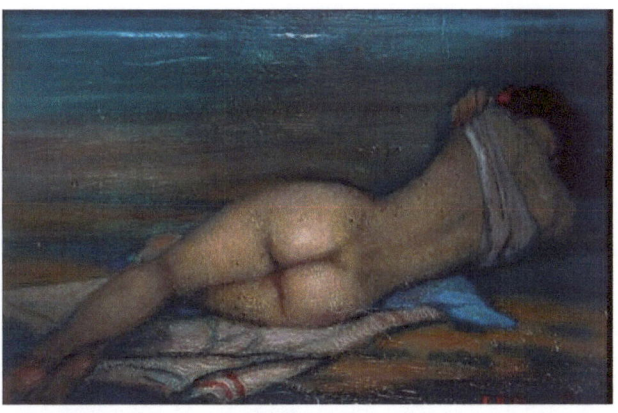

Nude--1915

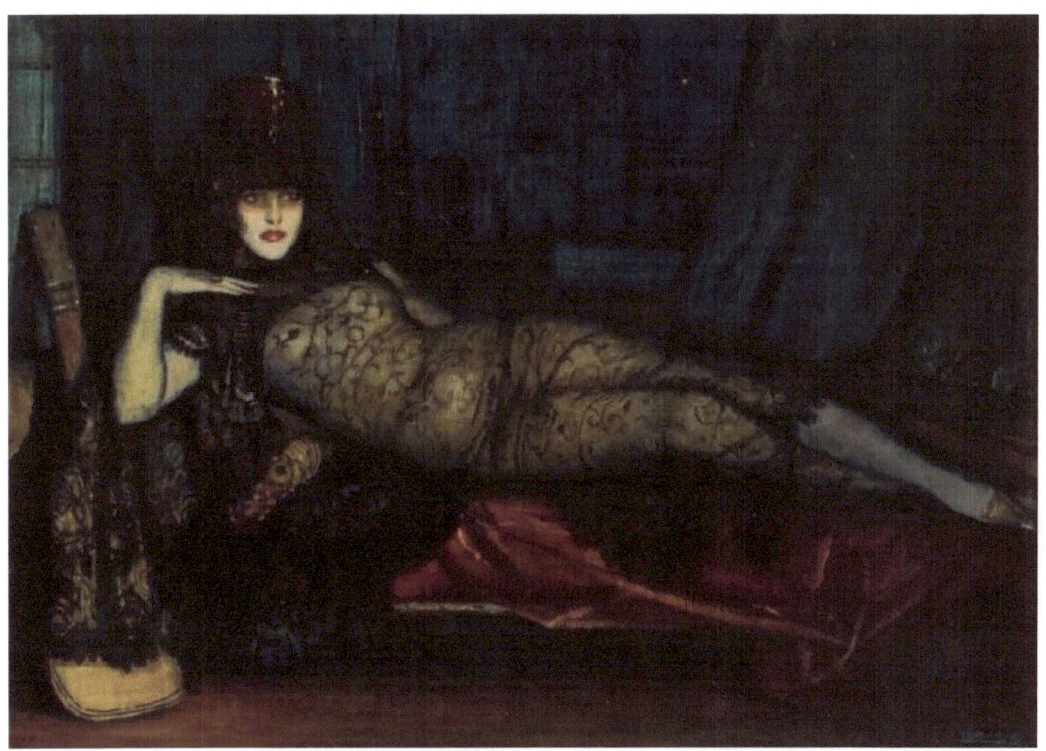

La Maja Maldita--1918

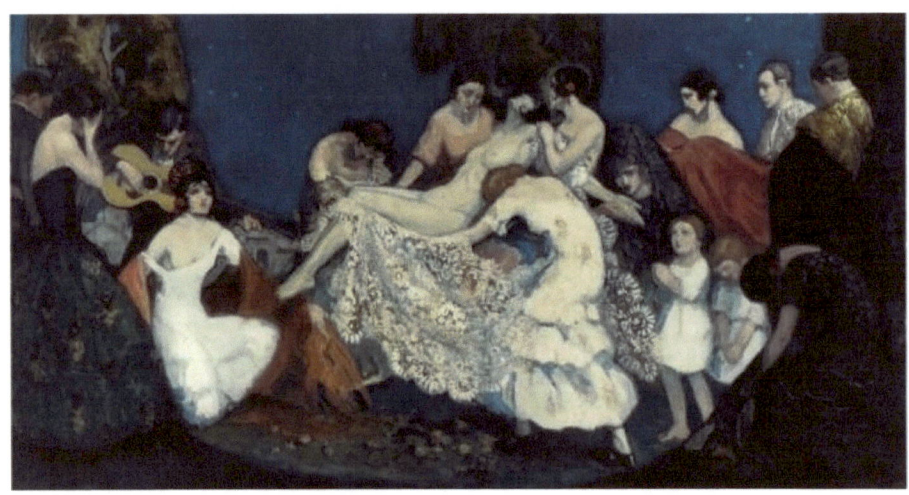

Allegory of Carmen--1916

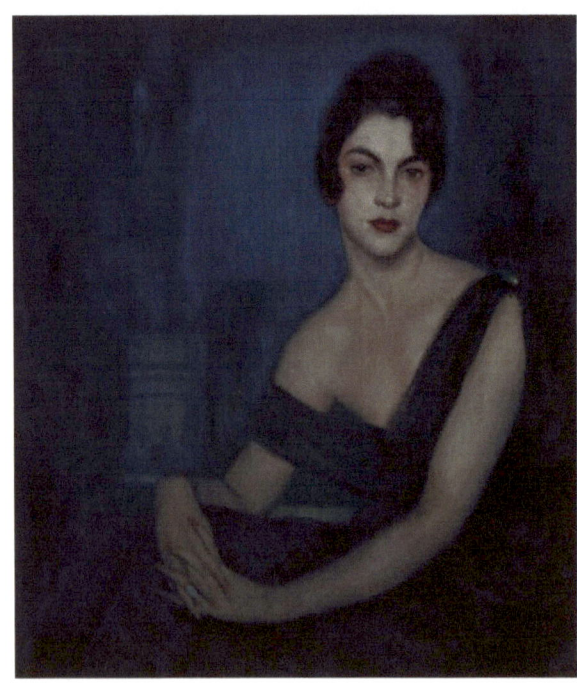

Portrait of Elegant Woman--1918

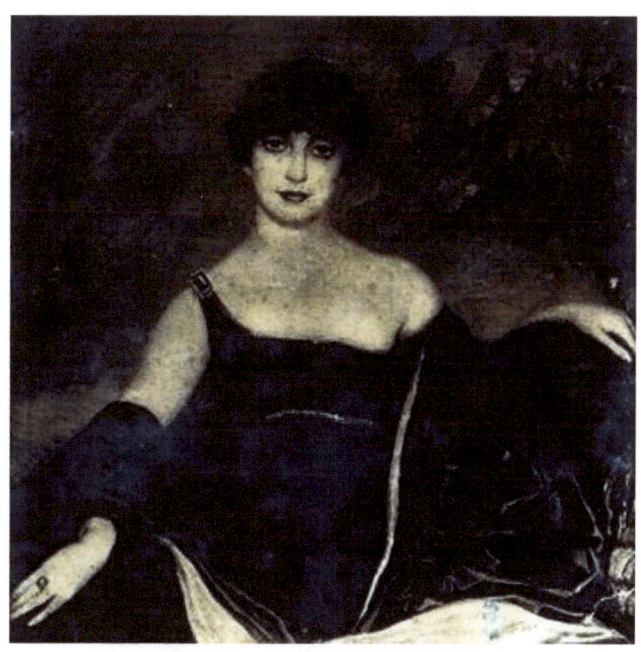

Portrait of an Elegant Woman

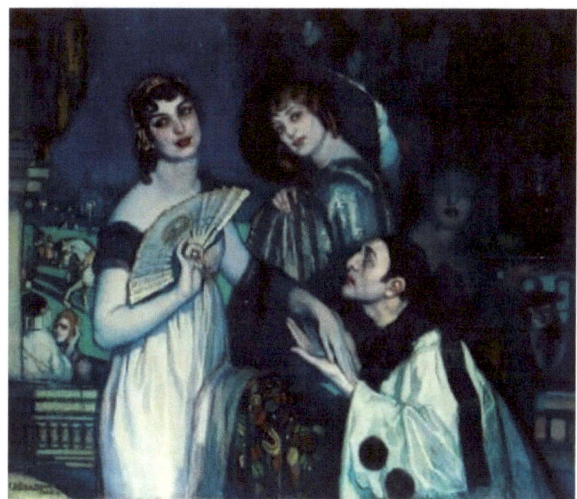

Blue Hour

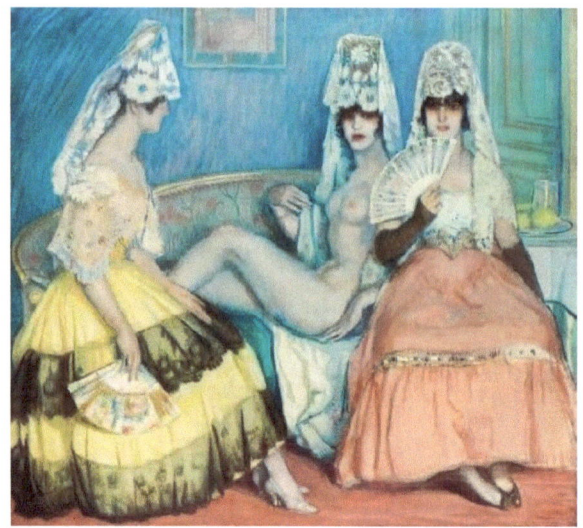

La Maja Marquesa, 1915

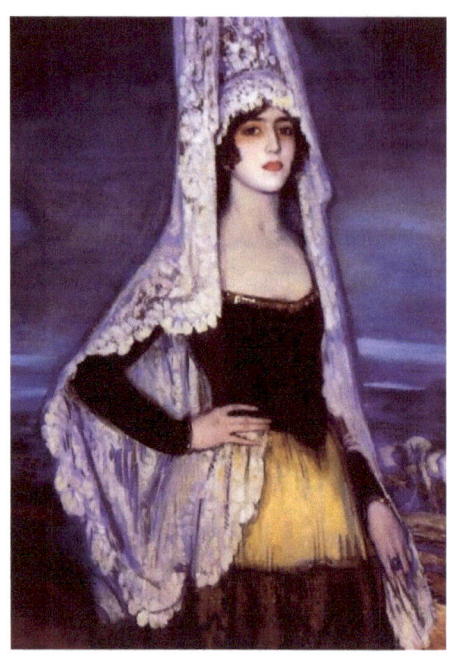

A Spanish Beauty--1934.

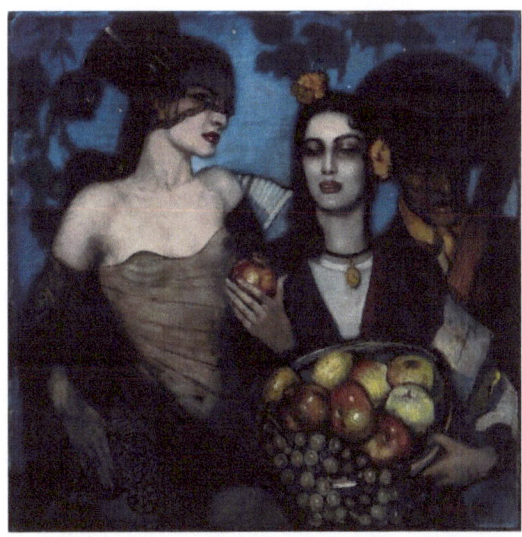

Granada

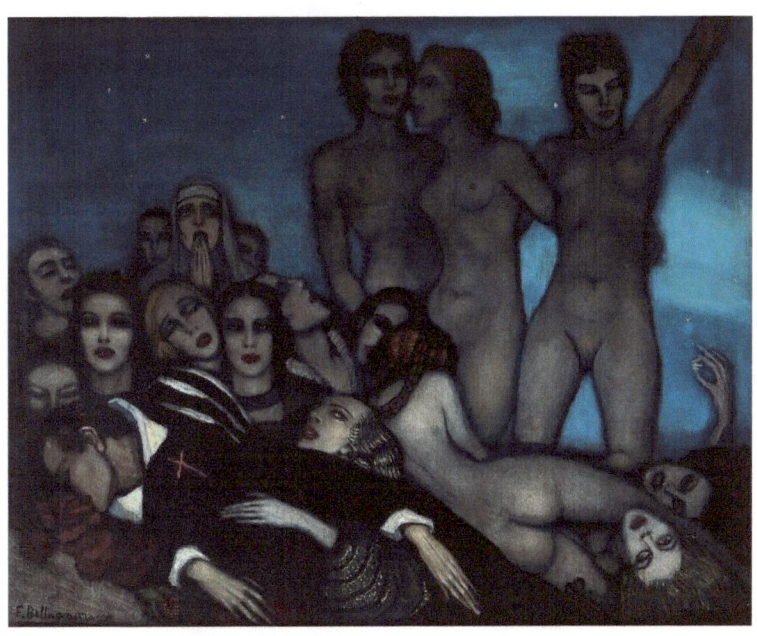

El sueño de don Juan--1938

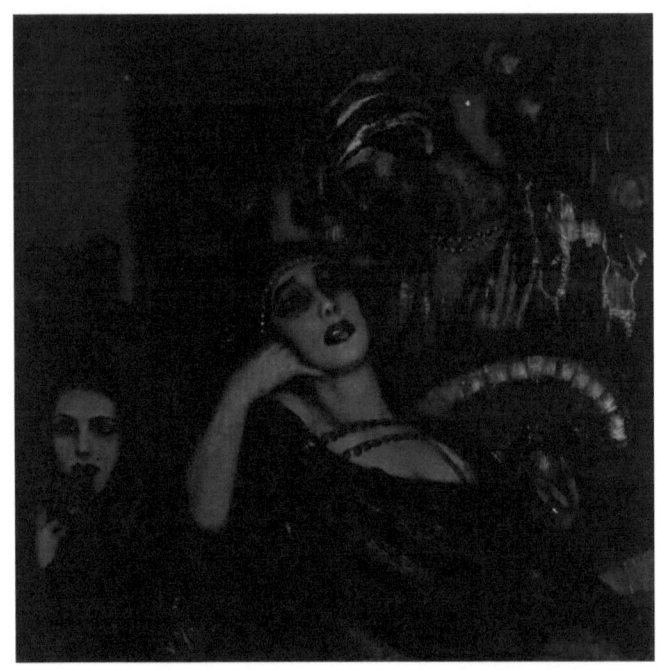

Le reve d'Oreste (la antigua Granada)--1919

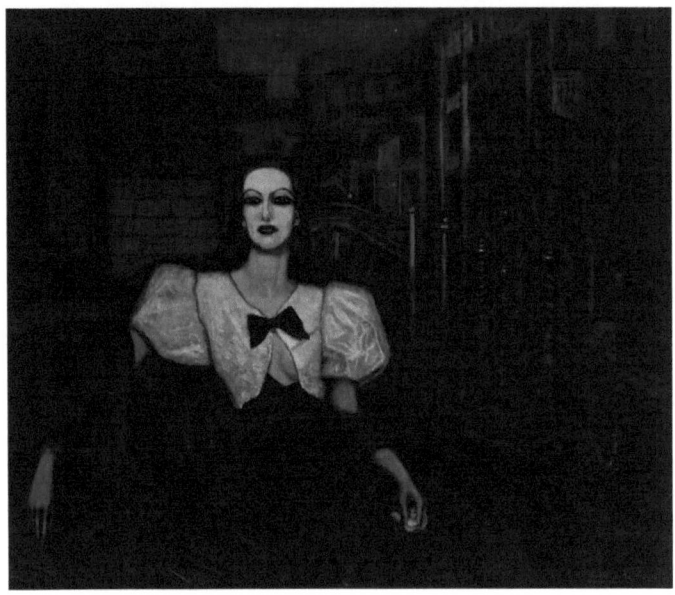

Miss Joan Crawford

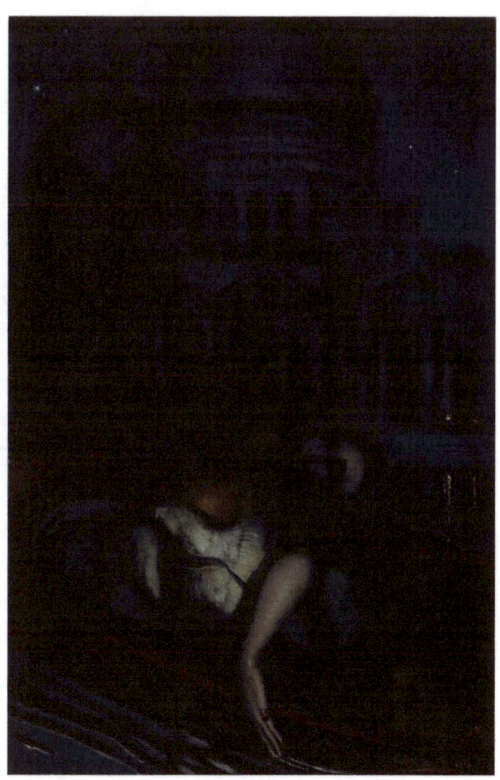

Pasión (Passion)

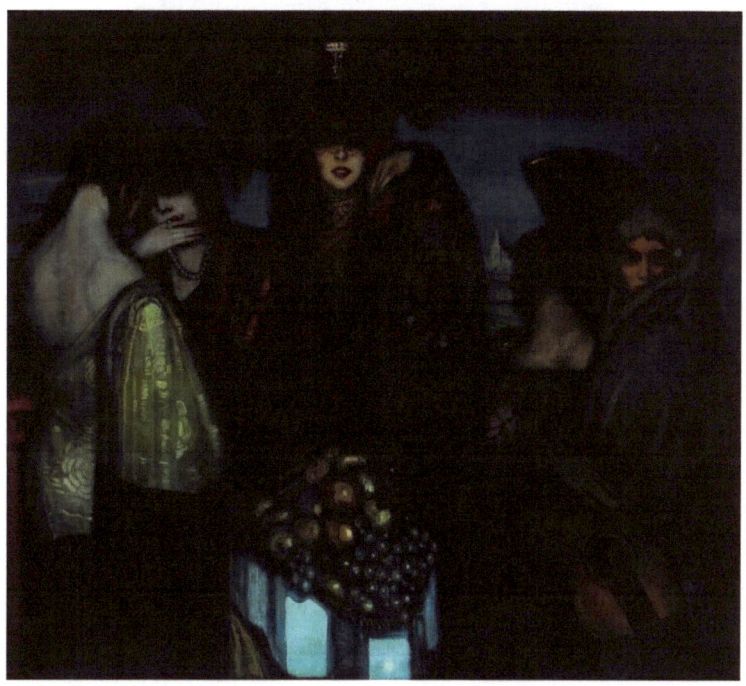

Las Ibericas (The Iberian Women)--1924

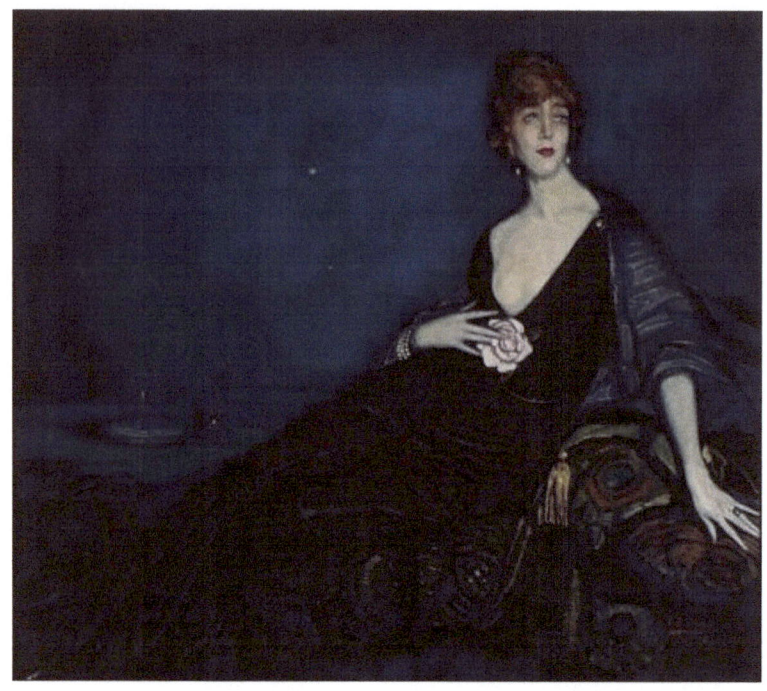

Mrs Freda Dudley Ward(later Marquesa de Casa Maury)--1921

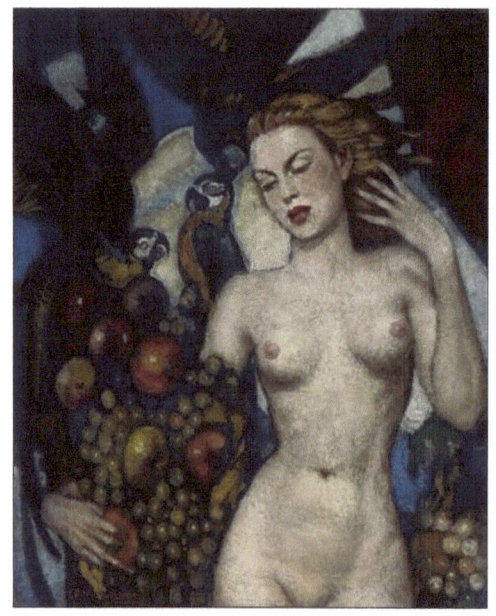

Tropical, 1925

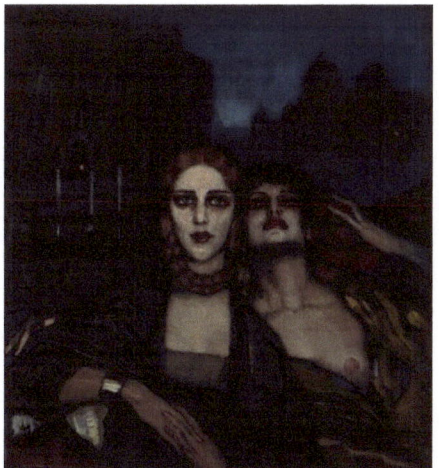

Las hermanas de Venecia (The Venetian Sisters)--1920

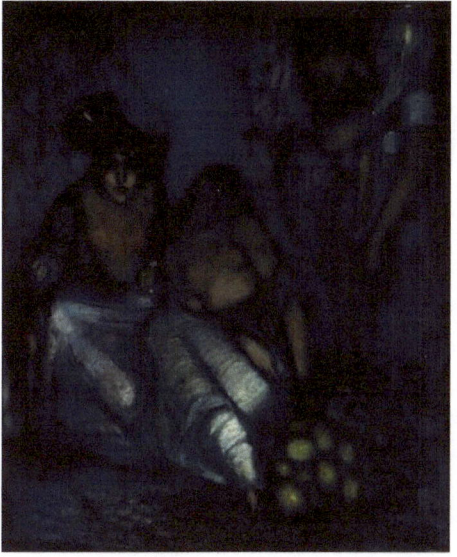

Los Limones (The Lemons)--1919

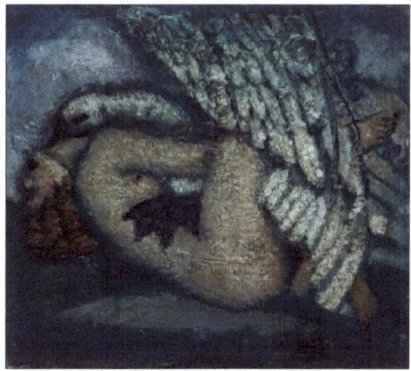

Leda y el Cisne (Leda and the Swan)--1917

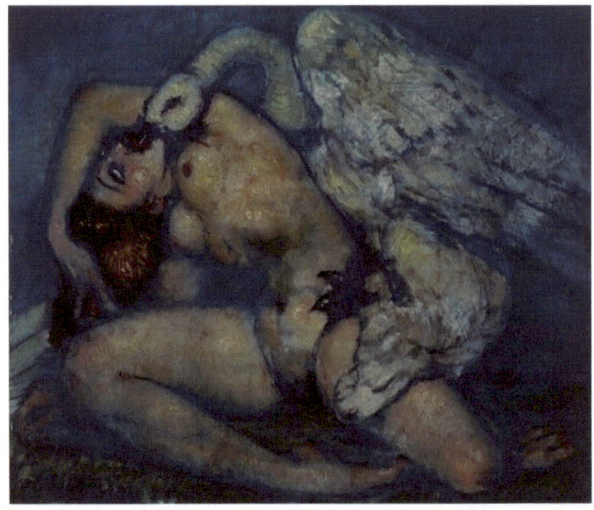

Leda y el Cisne (Leda and the Swan)--1917

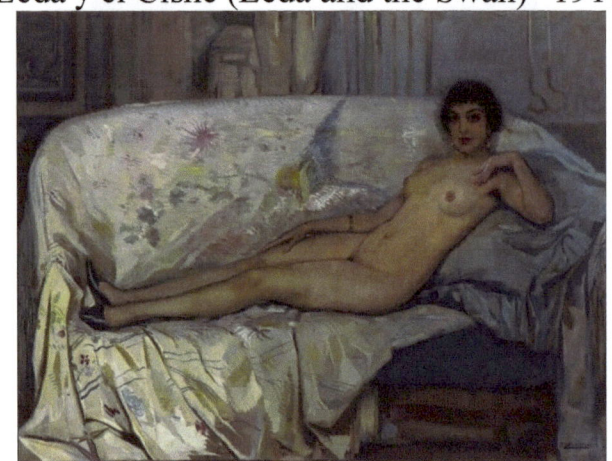

La Mirabella--1914

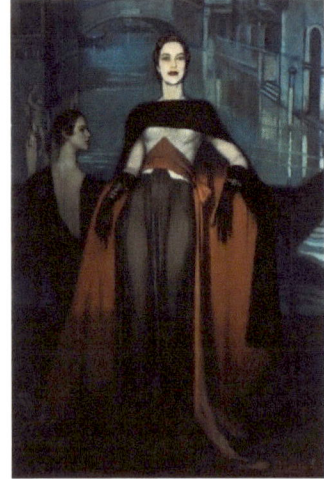

Federico La Condesa de Montgomery, Madame Bonnardel, 1934.

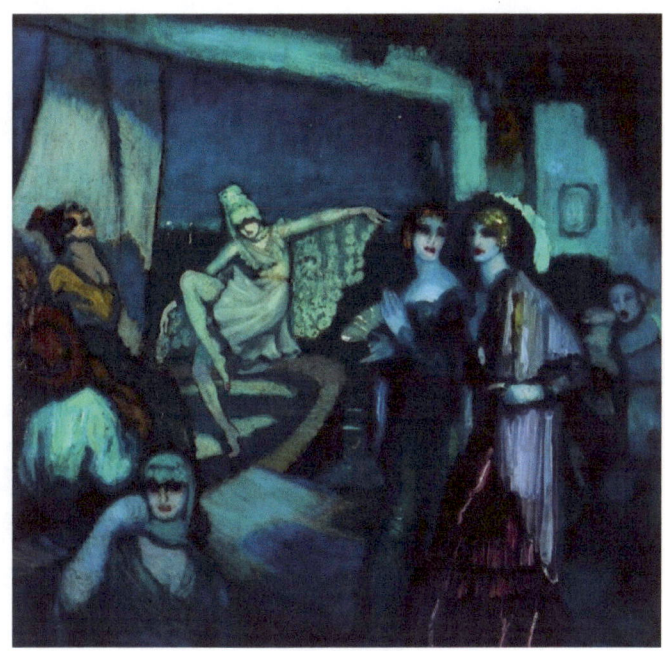

Carnaval

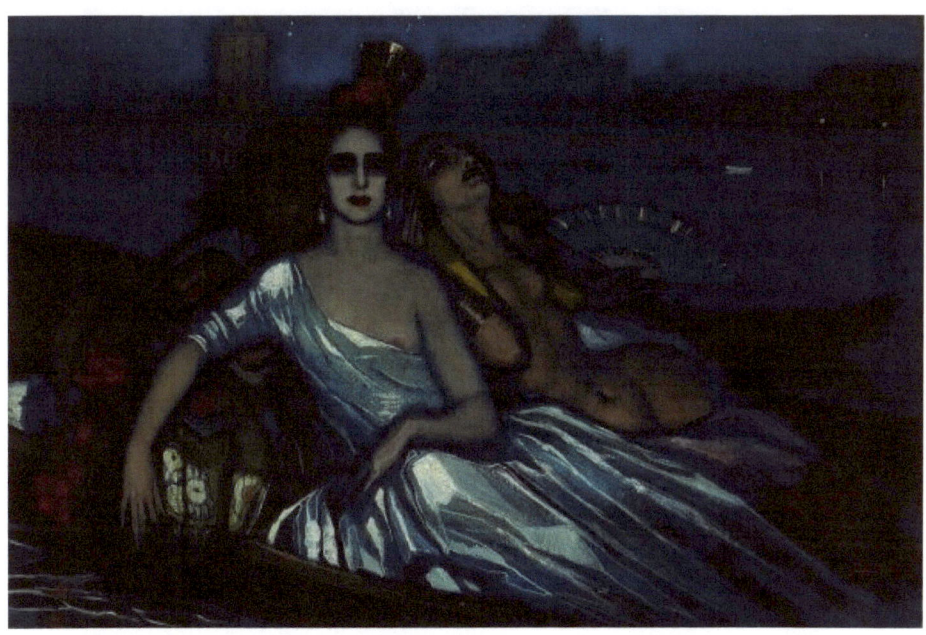

Muses on the Guadalquivir

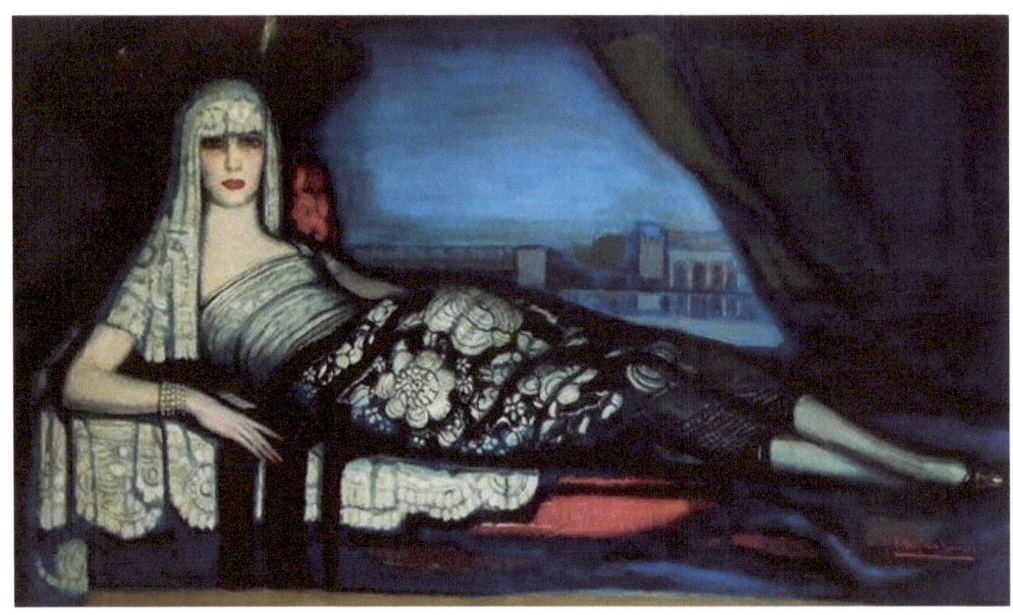

Femme Dans Le Chale Espagnol--.1925

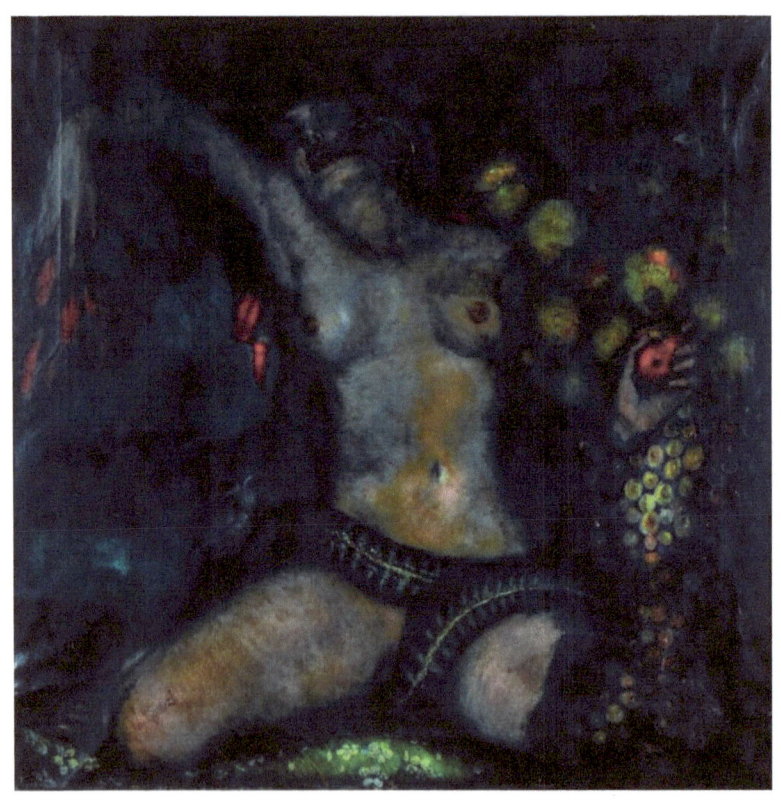

Eva--1929

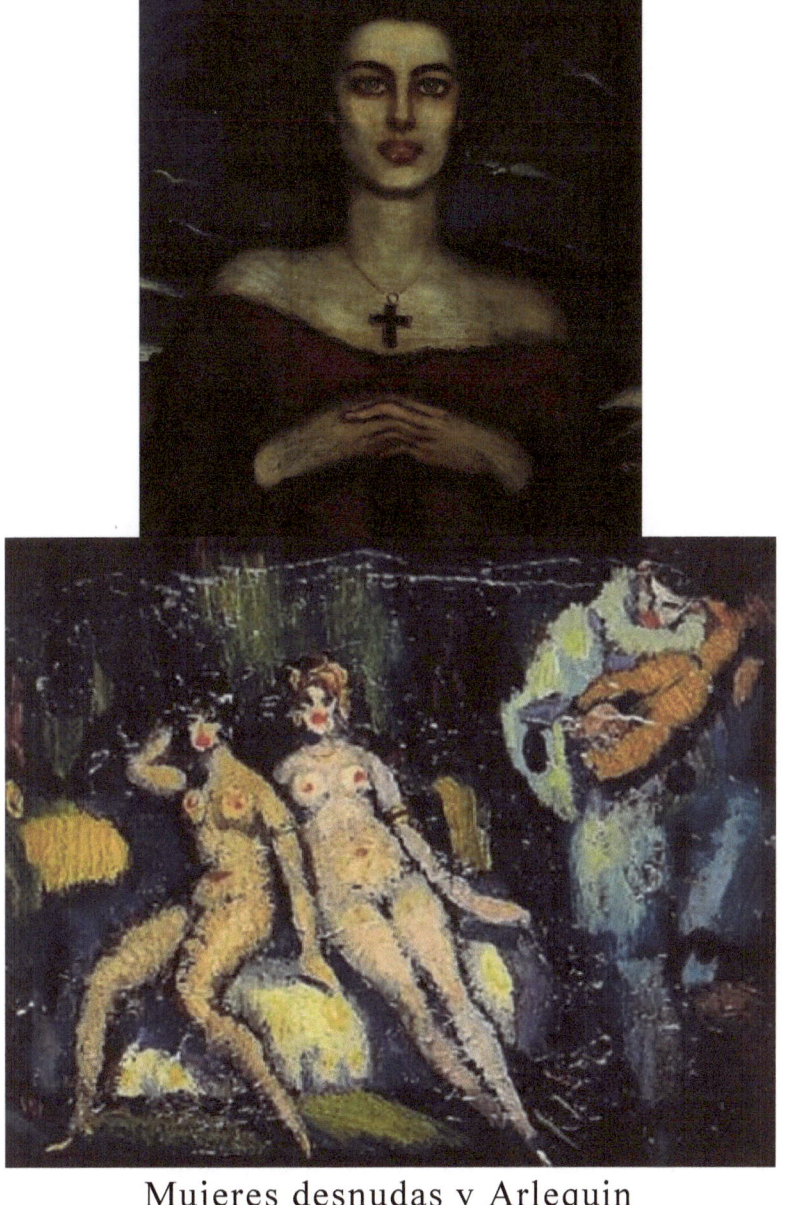

Mujeres desnudas y Arlequin

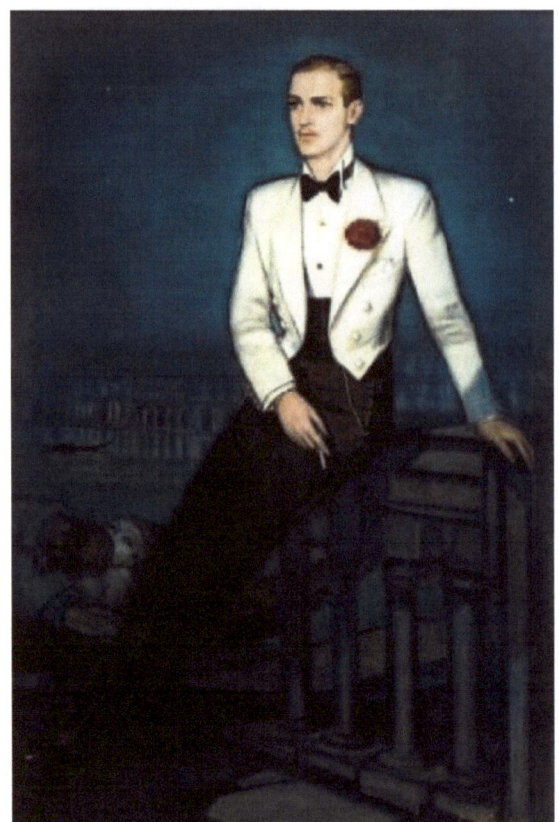

Douglas Fairbanks Jr.

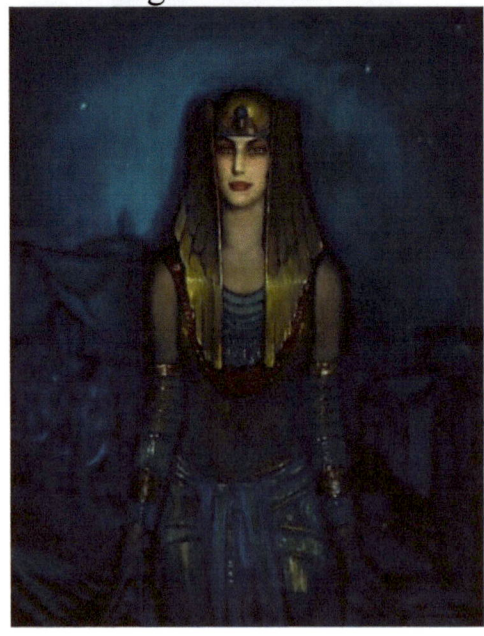

Blue Nights and Libertine Legends –

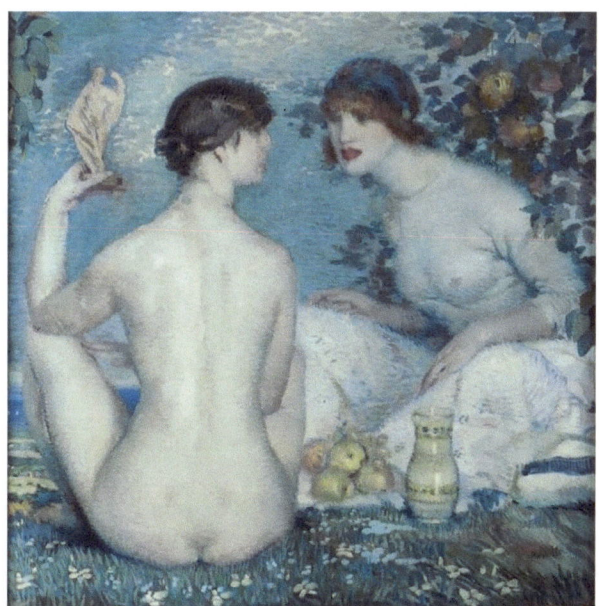

Tanagra, 1914

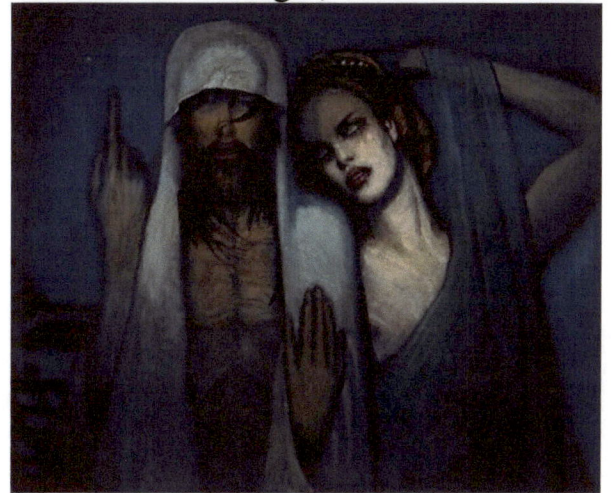

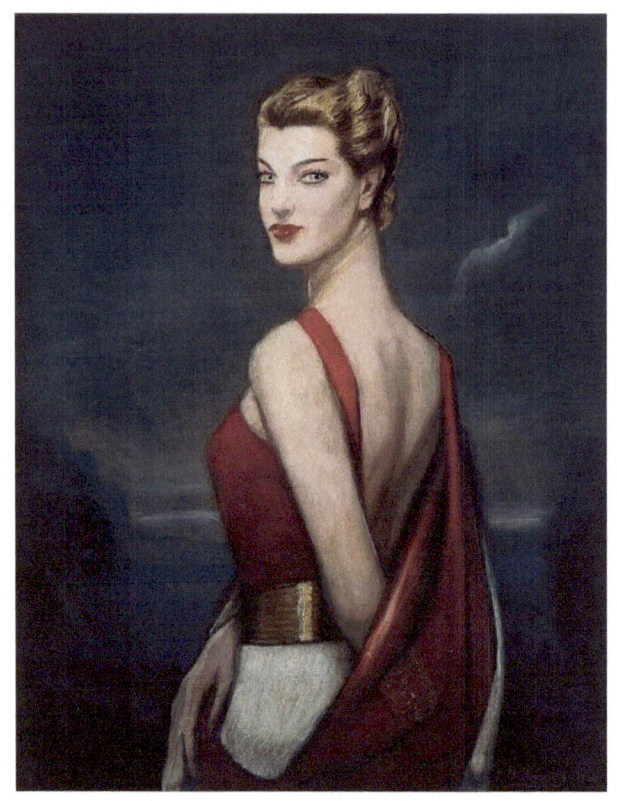

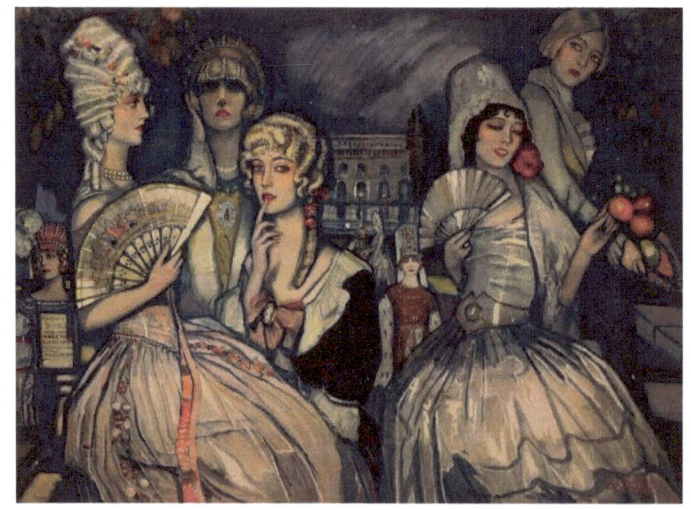

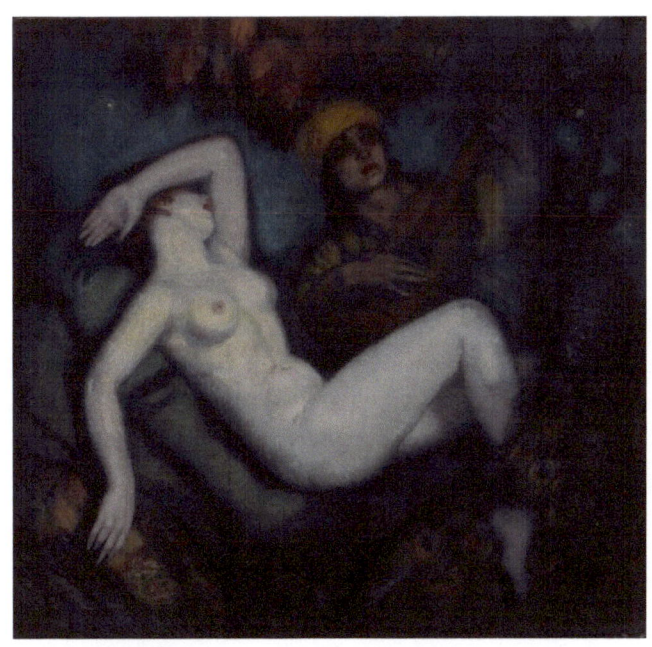

Invocación a Lackmy, 1914

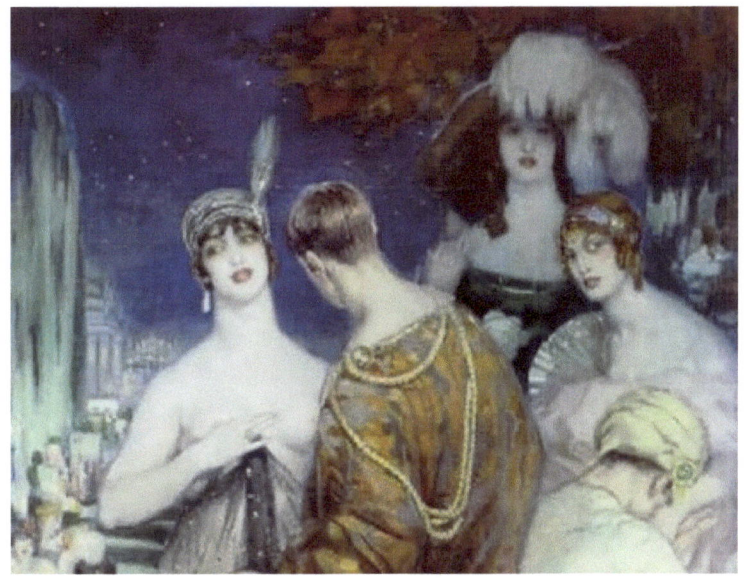

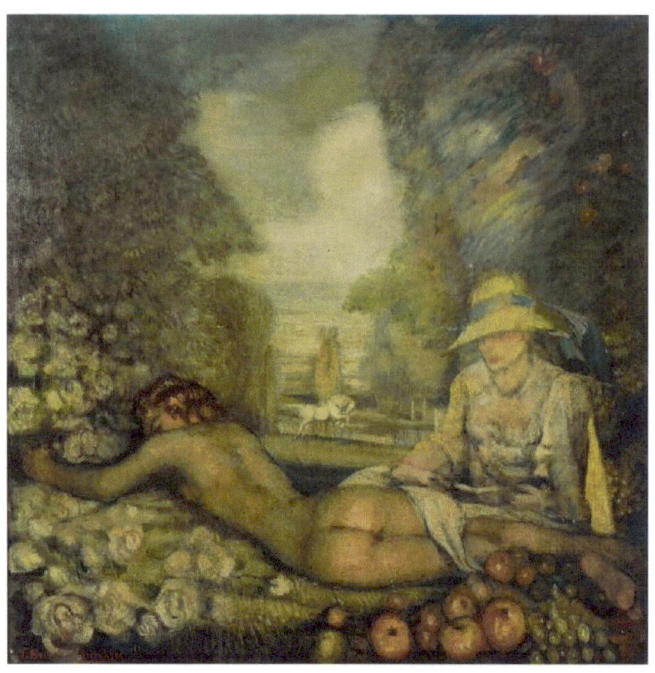

Le sommeil d'Eve

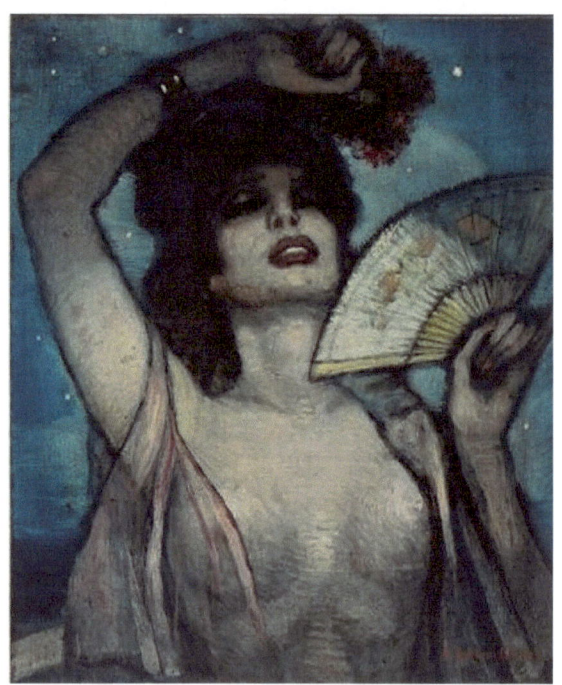

Young lady with fan

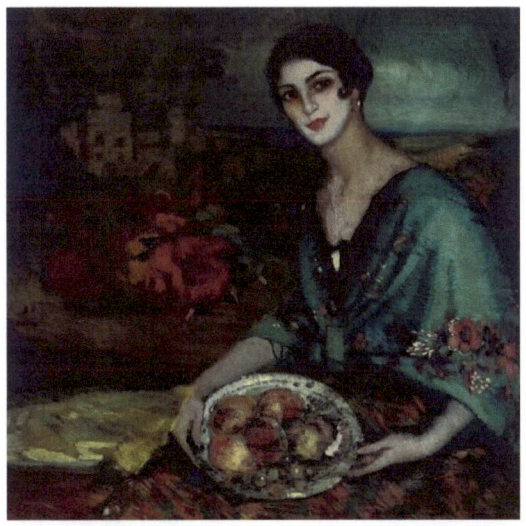

Mujer de azul (Woman in blue)

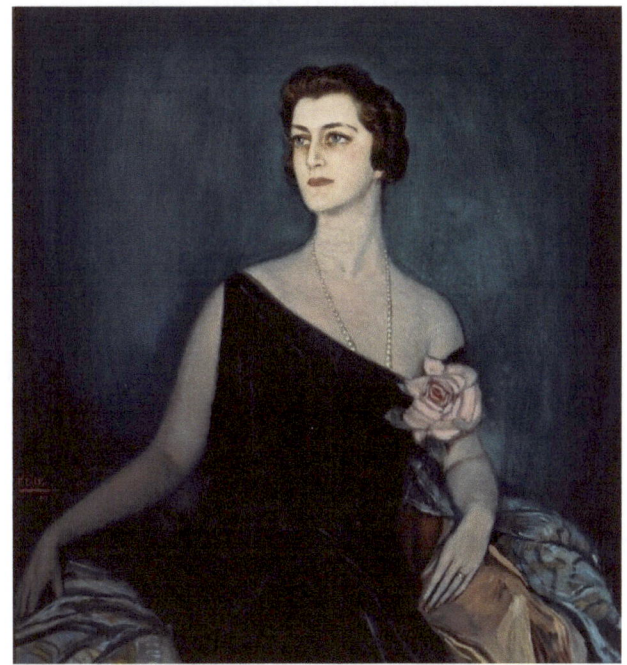

A portrait of May Fleishhacker

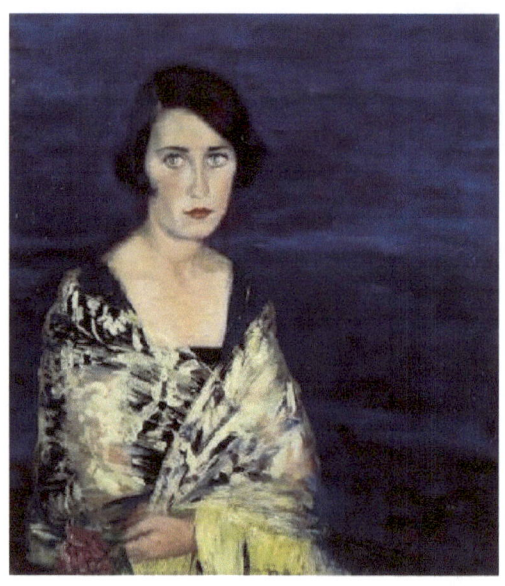

Portrait of a lady

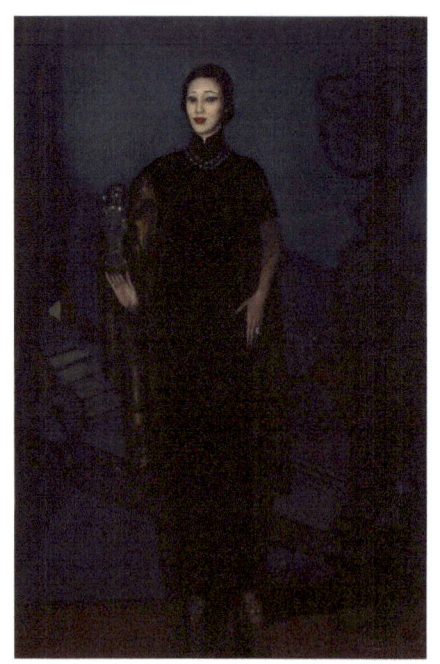

1934年，为黄蕙兰绘制的画像

From *Les Fleurs du mal (The Flowers of Evil)* which is a volume of
French poetry by Charles Baudelaire

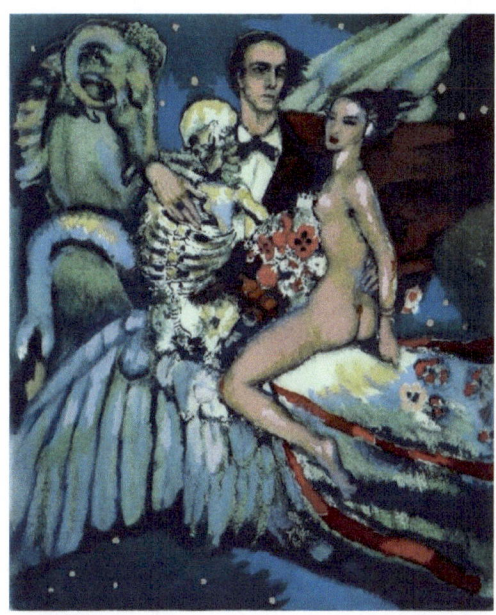

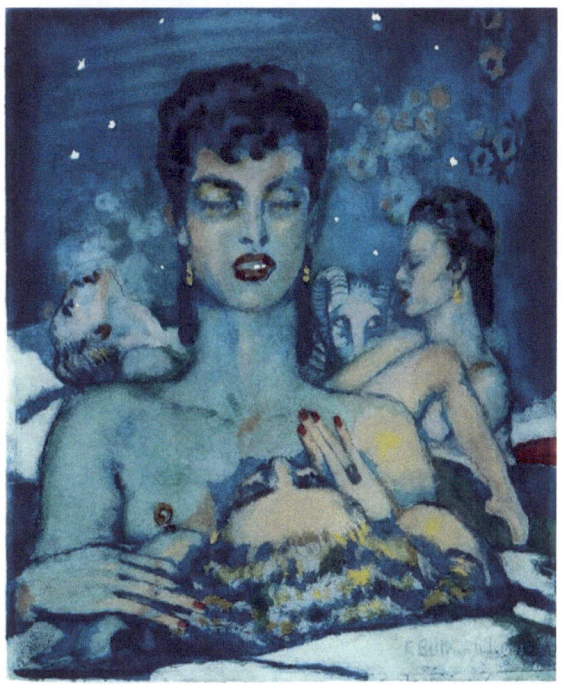

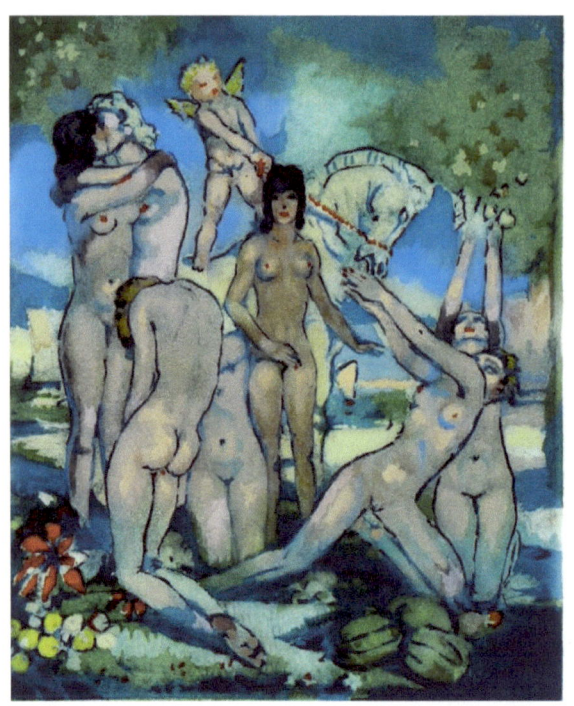

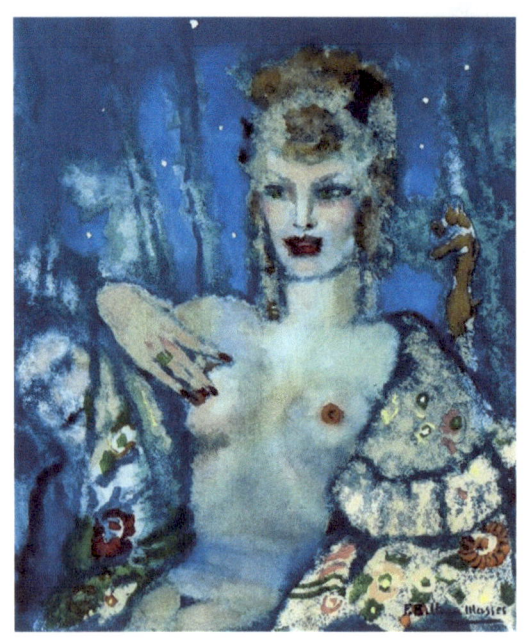

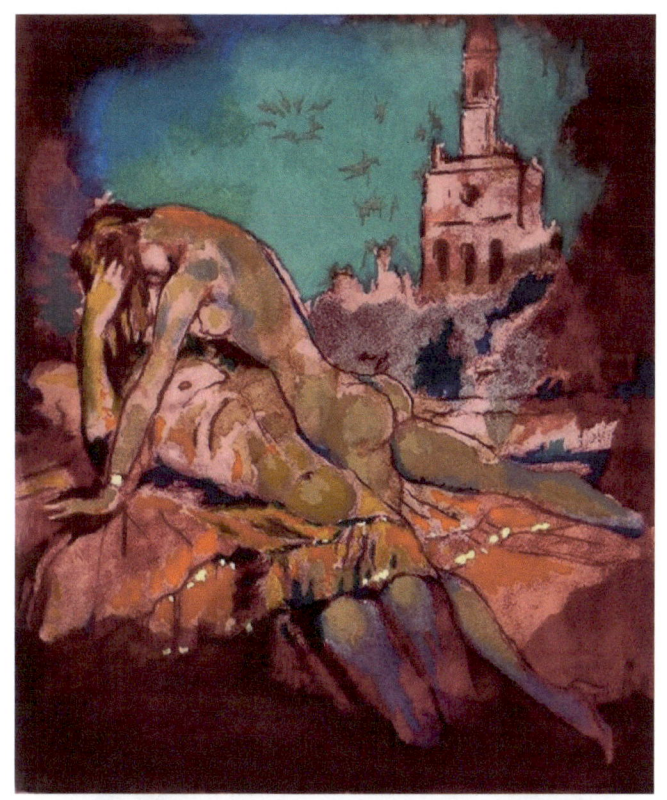

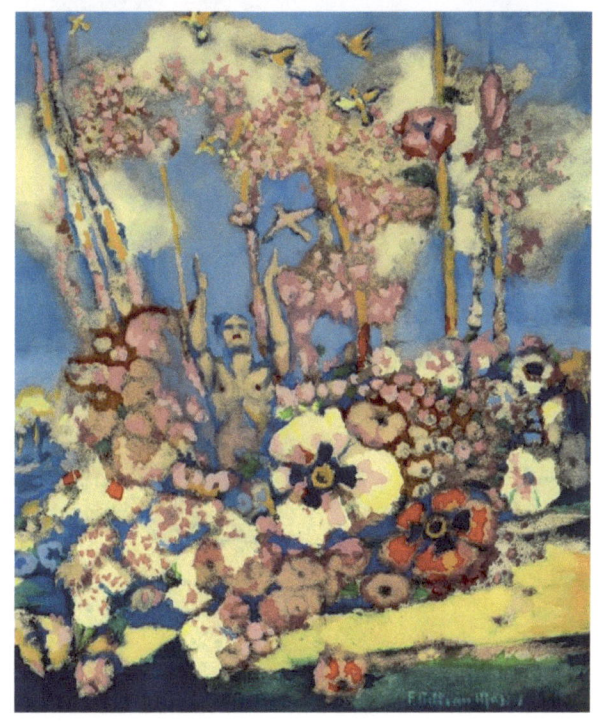

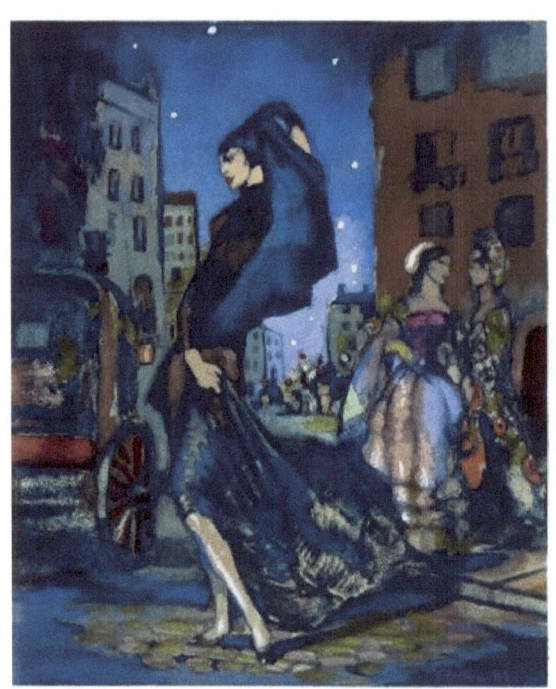

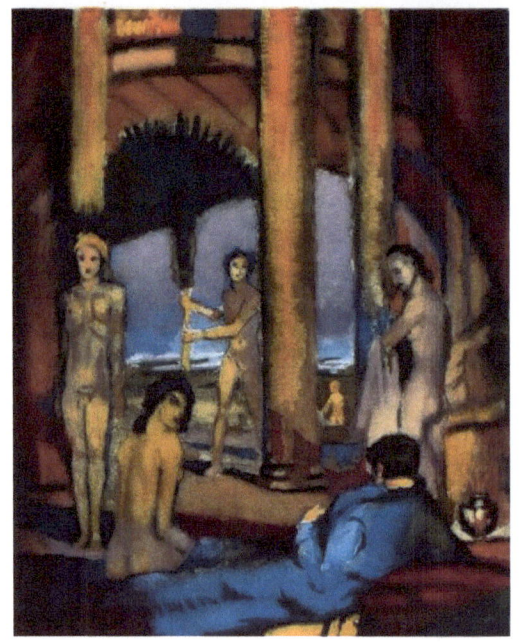

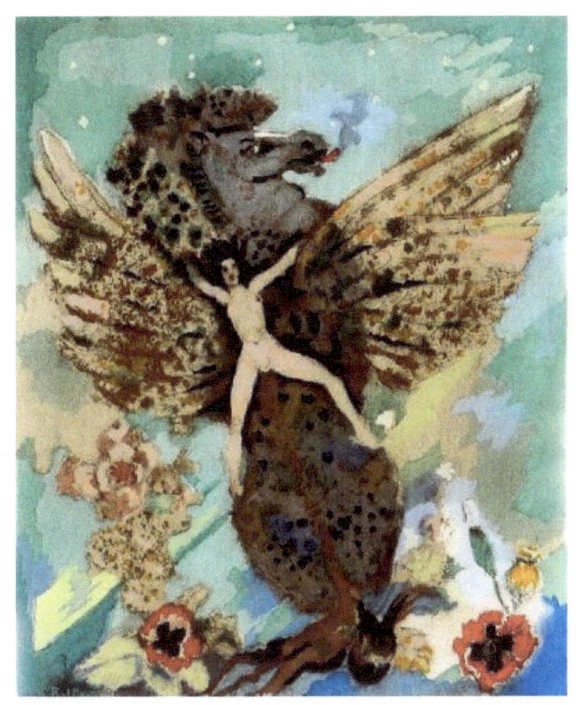

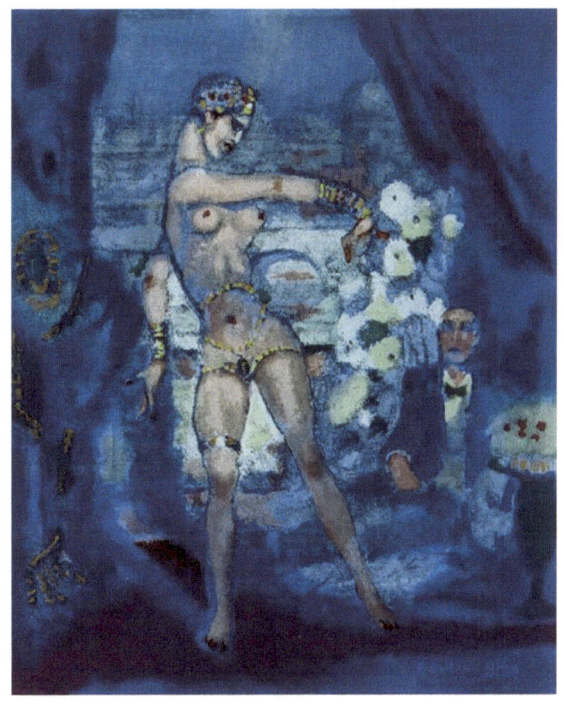

www.ingramcontent.com/pod-product-compliance
Lightning Source LLC
Chambersburg PA
CBHW040753200526
45159CB00025B/1945